DIAMONDS IN THE SURF

Bob Trevillian and Frank Carter

© Copyright 1982
Robert E. Trevillian III and Francis Carter
Spyglass Enterprises

Printed in the United States
All Rights Reserved
This book may not be reproduced
in whole or in part or in any
form without written permission
of the publisher.

Spyglass Enterprises
408 Arbor Drive, Glen Burnie, MD. 21061

*This book is dedicated
to our wives, Vicki and Barbara,
for their constant support and
unending encouragement.*

TABLE OF CONTENTS

CHAPTER 1
Beach Treasure 1

CHAPTER 2
The Equipment 11

CHAPTER 3
Tide and Weather Conditions 25

CHAPTER 4
The Hunt 33

CHAPTER 5
Researching Swimming Beaches 41

FOREWORD

Some say treasure hunters are born with it. That the desire for the search is in ones blood. I disagree. It has more of an addictive quality. Anyone who experiences the thrill of a treasure hunt can't help but be excited with the prospect of trying again.

Of course, finding lost or buried valuables is the final goal of all hunters. But the adventure and romance that can be experienced on the pathway to treasure surely rivals the thrill of locating the big bonanza. We can see evidence of this nearly every weekend when hunters head for the local park, detectors in hand, searching for a few old coins or perhaps a lost piece of jewelry. The monetary rewards are not always great, but the enjoyment and satisfaction of unearthing a part of history are rewards in themselves. In his own way a treasure hunter is also an amateur archeologist searching for articles lost and forgotten.

For most, the idea of recovering valuable treasure usually centers around the professionals, who scour the coast of Florida and the Carribean Islands in search of ancient spanish galleons. These vessels, now decaying wrecks hidden for centuries are sometimes laiden with gold doubloons, rare jewels and pieces of eight. But indeed they are rare and the tremendous expense of undertaking this type of search has left many investors penniless. The rewards can be great, but the odds are stacked against even the most experienced professional. Men who seek treasure wrecks are willing to risk it all for that one slim chance.

For the amateur, however, there is a facet of treasure hunting that is much less costly and can be extremely lucrative. I have enjoyed it for many years and the thrill is no less evident today than when I first experienced it. Perhaps the most primitive form is called beachcombing. But believe me, this ancient art of picking up assorted jetsom from the surf has come a long way.

New metal detectors designed to operate in shallow water have opened a new door to the recovery of lost coins and jewelry from swimming beaches. This book will introduce you to these new machines in addition to all the equipment useful to make your beach hunting profitable. Hunting the water also requires specific instruction on water conditions, searching techniques and ability to research and locate prime beach sites. The contents of this book has been compiled with years of experience. Not just years of searching but years of finding.

In the spring of 1981, co-author Frank Carter and myself were searching an abandoned beach along the Chesapeake Bay. The weather was quite stormy and the surf pounded the shore line, eroding vast amounts of sand. Even though the conditions were rough, we decided to hunt for a short period of time before leaving. Only one ring was found that afternoon, to be specific a diamond ring. It later was appraised for $13,000 and weighed 2.35 cts.

Of course, finds of this nature are rare, but they do exist. The constantly changing shoreline offers you an opportunity to tap into its vast amount of lost treasure. For those who look there are truly diamonds in the surf.

Bob Trevillian
March, 1982

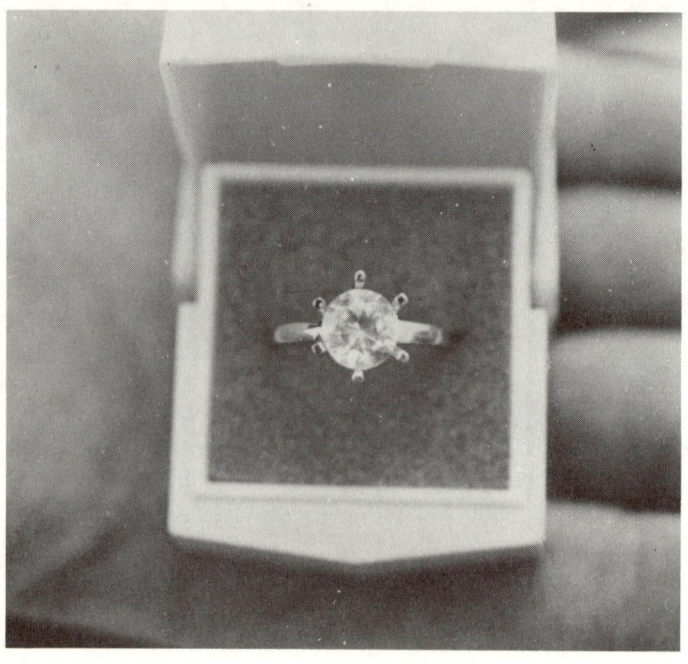

What a beauty!

CHAPTER 1

BEACH TREASURE

There's a basic scientific principal that most children are taught in grade school. It clearly states that when matter is heated it expands and when cooled it contracts. Fingers are no exception. They shrink in the cold of winter and swell in summer, sometimes very noticeably. That's why rings that we wear are often loose and at other times quite tight.

A finger doesn't need to contract very much in order to allow a ring to slip from the owner's possession. And nothing else affects the size of a finger more dramatically than cool water.

Common sense tells us that water temperature rarely exceeds the human body temperature of 98.6°F. Consequently, the cooler the water in relation to the body the more the finger will contract. Swimmers who remain in the water for a long period of time will show signs of "pruning", where their skin takes on a shriveled appearance, most noticeably in the toes and fingers. When this condition appears any sudden movement by the swimmer can easily cause a ring to slip away. Throwing a ball or frisby is a prime example.

Water also acts as a lubricant, adding another factor to the odds of losing jewelry at the beach. Between the effects of cool water on the size of a finger and its lubricating qualities, wearing a ring while swimming is a risky proposition at best.

Once that ring is lost, it's relatively impossible to retrieve it without the help of a metal detector. The bottom sand of a beach is constantly changing. Wind conditions and the effect of the tides causes the sand to move even though most swimmers will not even feel any change under their feet. An object can be covered in a matter of seconds and rings are capable of dropping much faster and deeper than articles with a flat surface. Picture a ring as a circular knife blade rapidly cutting down through the sand. Naturally, the heavier the ring the quicker it will sink. It's no wonder beach hunters have found so many valuable rings and assorted pieces of jewelry. What's truly amazing is the fact that people will continue to wear these items while swimming. The next time you visit the beach take a good look around at the swimmers who take a dip while wearing a ring, bracelet or necklace. A portion of what you see will be lost. What beach hunters have already found has proved this point time and time again.

Without a doubt the most common jewelry find is the school ring. Because school rings are so heavy and bulky they are easily lost. Let's face it, kids love the water. They don't swim just to cool off or for the sake of exercise. Kids go to the beach to have fun. they dive more and play active games.

Chicken fights are an all-time favorite and without a doubt have been responsible for quite a few rings lost in the heat of battle. It isn't unusual for a beach hunter to recover fifteen or more school rings on a good day. Since they usually contain more gold than most other rings, hunters consider them an especially good find.

Wedding bands are also found in great numbers, basically because so many people wear them. It's not unusual to find older bands containing over half an ounce of 18K gold. Wedding bands with diamonds turn up at times but not nearly as frequent as the plain variety.

Reason would tell us that expensive rings, mainly those displaying precious gemstones, would be few and far between. Responsible individuals would have more sense than to swim with a valuable piece of jewelry on their finger. But experience has proven otherwise. Many beach hunters have recovered up to ten diamond rings in a single day. Others can boast of finding as many as one hundred diamonds after searching a particular beach over a period of time.

Apparently, many swimmers enter the water and completely forget they are wearing jewelry. They may not even realize they have lost it for quite some time. Others know it instantly but then of course it's too late.

A good example took place a few years ago at a swimming beach on the Severn River in Maryland. A family travelling through the state in a large motor home decided to stop for a swim one afternoon. Apparently it was quite hot that day and they were very anxious to cool off. Within minutes they were enjoying the water with the rest of the swimmers. Later when the family decided to leave, the mother discovered the diamond she had treasured for so many years had slipped from her finger. In an emotional out-burst she urged the others on the beach to help her find the ring and offered a $500 reward to anyone who could recover it. The diamond was worth several thousands of dollars. No one collected the reward that afternoon and to anyone's knowledge the ring has never been found.

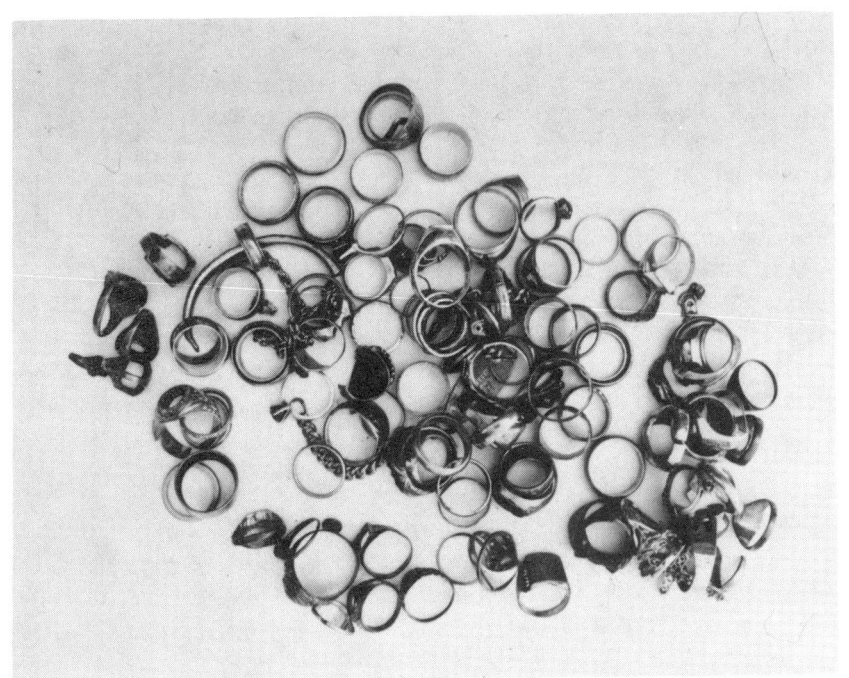

These gold rings were found all in one summer by a weekend beach hunter.

Since that afternoon, many beach hunters have searched this site in hopes of recovering that special ring. Even though it has continued to elude the most determined hunters by no means has their time been wasted. While searching they have recovered hundred of gold rings including a number of fine diamonds. It's a real thrill to be digging gold and silver knowing that at any moment an extremely valuable diamond may come to the surface. That beach will continue yielding treasure as long as people swim there and sooner or later some lucky hunter will find that diamond in the process.

There's no question that finding rings is the main goal of the beach hunter, but by no means are rings the only treasure that a swimming site will yield. As far as jewelry is concerned, necklaces can be found frequently. Apparently the clasp holding the chain around the swimmers neck either breaks or comes undone. Occasionally a link on the chain will snap while a swimmer is diving.

Sterling chains with religious medals are found in great numbers. St. Christopher medals, crucifixes and the Mother Mary are examples.

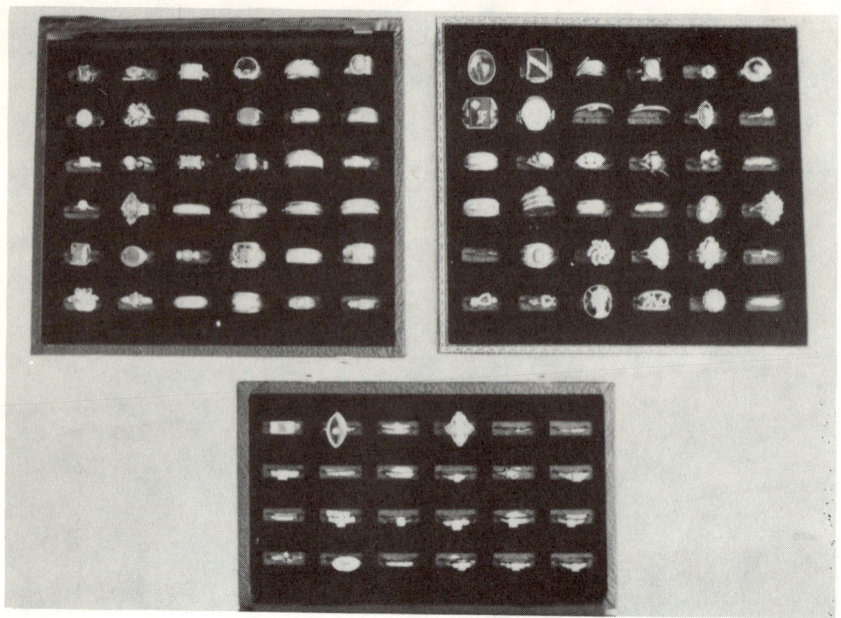

From the author's personal collection and appraised at over thirty thousand dollars.

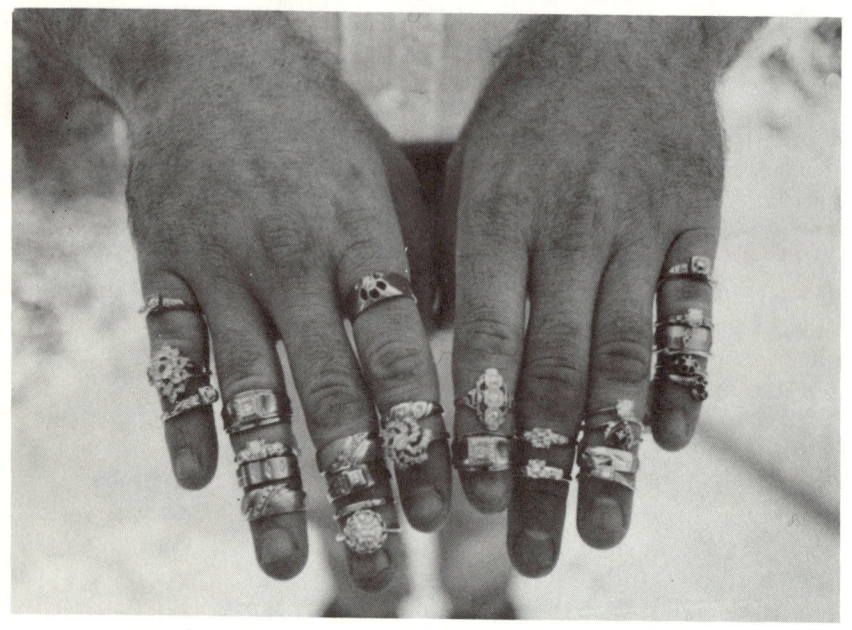

Quite a collection and they're all diamonds.

These types of medals were especially popular in the 50's and 60's and beaches that were active during these years bear this out.

Gold chains are far more difficult to find. From beach hunting experience it's obvious that gold chains and necklaces are not frequently worn in the water. In fact, it seems that far more diamond rings are recovered than gold chains. Perhaps the answer to this lies in the fact that most people wear their diamonds literally around the clock but gold chains and necklaces are worn primarily for dress occasions. Even so, if a swimmer wears a chain there's a very good chance it will be lost, basically due to the fragile workmanship in this type of jewelry.

Believe it or not, people actually wear watches and bracelets while swimming and lose them constantly. Fortunately for the beach hunter most watches manufactured today are waterproof and are capable of surviving in running condition for a reasonable amount of time before sand and water finally damage their inner workings. The shifting sands of ocean and bay beaches are a powerful force and over a period of time even the most rugged time pieces cannot withstand this kind of beating. But remember, many watches manufactured in the past were made of solid gold. Even though they are found with the inner workings ruined by water action, the precious metal value is still there.

There was a time not too long ago that identification bracelets were about as popular as apple pie. It seemed that every teenager wore one with either their own name or their boyfriend or girlfriend's name engraved across the top. Often bought as a gift, the most popular style was made of sterling silver and most were quite heavy. It isn't unusual to find an ID bracelet weighing well over 3 ounces. This certainly makes a bracelet an excellent find for the beach hunter.

That's exactly what makes treasure hunting beaches so great. Jewelry finds are not the exception, but rather the rule. It's hard to convince someone who has never ventured into the water with a metal detector that these finds are possible. Most coin shooters have only searched the beach where the bathers sprawl out to catch a few rays of the sun. This isn't to say that treasure cannot be found there, but compared to what lies in the surf and beyond, the finds are miniscule. It isn't an exaggeration to say that for every article lost on the beach, there are at least ten lost in the water itself. As you read earlier, the odds of losing jewelry and other valuables increases dramatically when someone leaves the beach and decides to take a swim.

Recently the proprietor of a popular beach on the Chesapeake Bay revealed that on an average day as many as fifteen people report the loss of a piece of jewelry, mainly rings. It boggles the imagination to think of the volume being lost during the swimming season and especially the

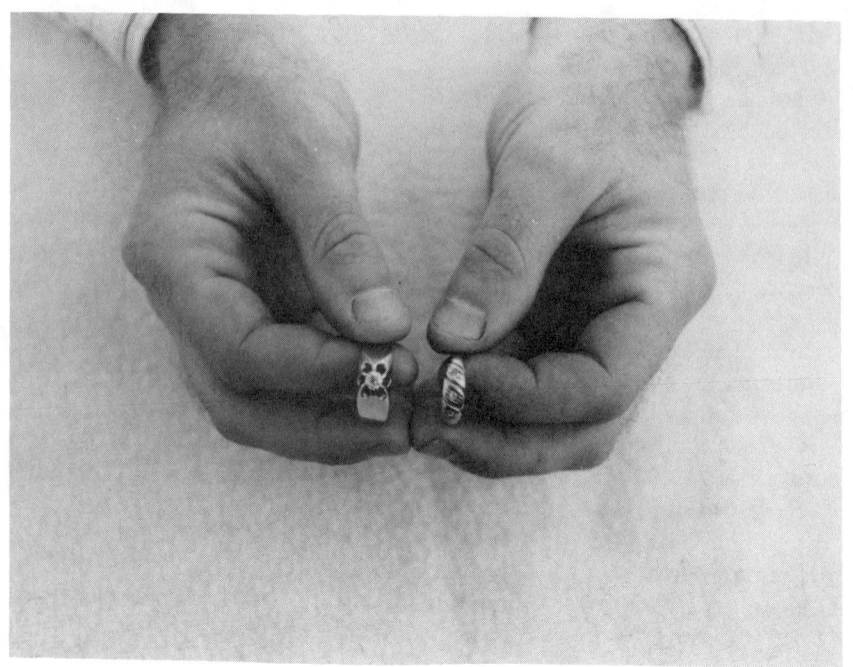

Two diamond rings found at the same beach, by the same hunter within five minutes.

tremendous amount of treasure lost over the past years, waiting to be recovered by the beach hunter.

Beaches also contain an abundance of old coins. Somehow it seems unusual for a swimmer to carry coins into the water, but never-the-less they must, because the amount that turns up is staggering, especially silver coins. Remember, when Roosevelt instituted the New Deal program in the early 30's, he began building parks and recreational facilities across the nation. Many of these parks included swimming beaches and quickly became popular resort areas for the average family that experienced financial difficulties due to the depression. Of course, silver coins were in circulation up until 1964. That's over thirty years of possible lost silver. And that silver sure has turned up in many a beach hunter's collection.

In some parts of the country where gambling had been legal in the past, some resort owners constructed extensive piers where dozens of one arm bandits were lined up for those who wished to try their luck.

Of course, these piers were also well supplied with alcoholic beverages that helped to coax the gambler to put a bit more in the machine. Many

Gold and silver medalians recovered while beach hunting.

The remains of a pier constructed for gambling.

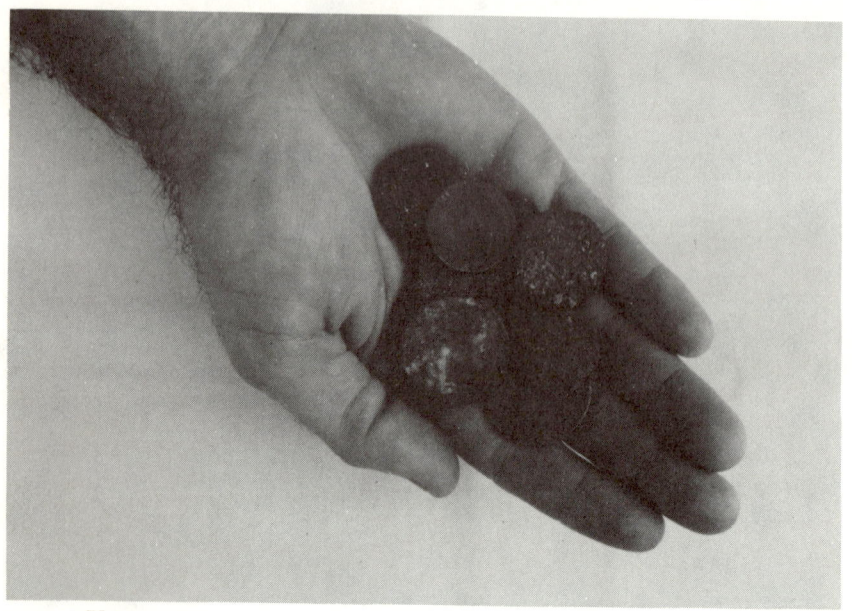

An assortment of silver coins recovered from swimming sites.

Silver coins, black with oxidation, as they look when recovered from salt water.

of these bandits even accepted half dollars, but the usual wager was either a nickel or quarter.

As you might expect, beach hunters have had great success beneath these piers. Literally several thousands of silver coins were lost at a typical gambling beach. Silver halves, mainly of the Walking Liberty variety are found in unusually high quantities. But this isn't to say that coins aren't found at the average recreational beaches. They are indeed. In fact many hunters have recovered coins dating back to the mid 1800's.

Unlike today's more fashion minded swimwear, bathing suits of the past were made to include a small pocket where swimmers could keep coins or most any small object while taking a dip. Unfortunately, the button that held the pocket closed often came undone or the pocket material came apart due to wear. And it certainly must have happened often as evidenced by the amount of coins that have been recovered in the water.

One particular beach hunter who has been active in the water over the last five years has a knack for finding change purses filled with coins. Somehow they survive the water currents and remain intact without spilling their contents. Most of these purses have held only silver coins. This just goes to show the extensive and varied amount of treasure that can be found where people swim.

Aside from finding a cache of valuables or locating a ship wreck, there are very few, if any, forms of treasure hunting as lucrative as searching swimming beaches. In fact, it may be surprising but it is possible to recover items considered antiques and collectables. Lead soldiers, radio and television premiums, and even old Cracker Jack toys are just a few of the possibilities. The popularity of these kinds of items has increased dramatically over the years. It seems these days everyone collects something, especially the articles that can be found so frequently at old beaches. Kids are notorious for jamming their pockets full of assorted play things and kids were no different fifty years ago. They loved to take toys in the water while swimming and naturally lost them quite often. Remember, these finds are no longer considered junk. They are quite valuable to collectors across the country and will become even more valuable in the future.

Perhaps what separates beach hunting most from any other form of treasure hunting is the fact that as long as people swim there will always be lost valuables. Yes, of course people lose items on the dry land but the ratio between land and beach is astronomical. Most anyone who has searched on land for treasure and also searched in the waters of a swimming beach will tell you the odds of routinely recovering any

A number of collectables, including skeleton keys, lead soldiers, tokens and Cracker Jack prizes.

articles of substantial value are tremendously higher when a hunter ventures into the water.

Although metal detectors have been available for decades, only recently has detector electronics come of age. Metal detectors are now being manufactured with a much higher level of versatility. They can easily be adpated for water searching, a task that was quite difficult years ago. In fact, a number of detector manufacturers now offer machines specifically made to hunt underwater.

These new steps in technology have opened a new door for the treasure hunter. It's a real opportunity to search for big time treasure without investing staggering sums of money into lavish equipment. And best of all, it's not difficult to become an expert hunter. With a little bit of determination and the right preparation, literally anyone can become successful. Not just a treasure hunter — but a treasure finder!

CHAPTER 2

THE EQUIPMENT

The science of Darwin tells us that mankind evolved from the oceans. That as fish we enjoyed the tranquil waters of prehistoric times but later decided to pursue an existence on land for some unknown reason. True or not true, we no longer resemble our so-called ancestors, nor do we fair very well when we return to our so-called original environment. Either way we are definitely fish out of water.

Treasure hunters have certainly experienced a great deal of difficulty while trying to master the problems of searching underwater. It's not an easy transition when a hunter decides to walk from land to water with a metal detector in hand. But fortunately for the newcomer, the basic experimenting is now over and the techniques for searching swimming beaches have been reasonably perfected.

Preparation is the real key to successfully mastering the beach. And good preparation means putting together the proper equipment. Aside from the metal detector most of the equipment a hunter needs can be homemade at minimum expense. In fact, it's doubtful that a prospective hunter could purchase all the equipment needed in prefabricated form. After all beach hunting is quite specialized and also relatively new. Perhaps in the future manufacturers will produce all the gear needed and might even package the entire all-in-one kit. That remains to be seen. But for now, aside from the detector, it's basically a do-it-yourself operation.

DIVING vs. WADING

Both diving and wading can be used successfully to search swimming beaches. However, there are a few good reasons why wading is a bit more practical for the average hunter. First of all, at the majority of swimming sites the bottom does not drop off too quickly to make wading impossible. In fact during low tide a hunter can wade out quite a

Using hip waders, a simple hand held detector and scoop, hunter searches the shoreline.

distance before encountering deep water. And from experience, this area where levels remain below the neck is where the majority of treasure is recovered. Lake and ocean beaches may drop off a bit faster, but there is still plenty of room to search without having to go underwater.

In most parts of the USA visibility below water is not very good. This causes quite a lot of difficulty when a diver attempts to retrieve a lost article after he has located it with a metal detector. Without seeing the bottom clearly it becomes a groping game where the hunter must rely heavily on feel. Many divers do it successfully but it's not an easy technique to master.

In addition, the equipment needed to dive is by no means inexpensive. Most states also require a diver to be certified in order to have scuba tanks filled by dealers. By the time a prospective hunter enters the water he has invested a healthy amount of cash.

After beach hunting for awhile, an individual may decide to pursue the diving angle. But its definitely a better bet to start with the simple technique of wading. But if you're like most treasure hunters, you will probably find that lost valuables found while wading are plentiful enough without ever having to venture underwater.

WADERS AND WET SUITS

It's sometime in January and a steady snowfall turns the sandy beach into a blanket of white. Although the air testifies to the frigid temperatures the salt water remains free, but dangerously close to freezing. A hooded figure can be seen a stones throw from the shoreline moving methodically among the wavelets.

Some would call him a die-hard. But the diamond ring now tucked safely in his pouch proves to the contrary. And although the waters are deathly cold he is quite warm and comfortable in his dive suit.

Sound a bit dramatic? Maybe, but in areas around the country where the winters are not overly harsh and the inland waters do not freeze over constantly, hunters pack their gear and head for the beaches year round.

The problem here is body protection. And the solution lies in the use of hip waders, chest waders, the wet suit or the dry suit. Each in it's own right does the job but in varying degrees of success depending on temperature and depth of water.

First of all, not all hunters wear protective gear. During the summer when the water becomes warm and comfortable, a tee-shirt and a pair of shorts will suffice. Of course, because a hunter is doing quite a lot of digging some sort of shoe has to be worn even if it's a simple pair of sneakers. And in areas of the country where the beaches are swimmable year round he may never have to worry about heavy gear.

There is one exception to warm weather hunting that may at least force a hunter to wear long pants, sweat shirt and plastic gloves. In other words, he must cover all parts of the body that remain exposed underwater. In some parts of the country and during certain times of the year, sea-nettles or jelly fish suddenly become a menace. These seemingly docile creatures can inflict quite a burn on human skin. They can easily be seen floating near the surface sporting an array of long tentacles. Just a quick contact with jelly fish can cause quite a bit of enduring pain.

The most basic form of body protection against cold water is a pair of hip waders. They are constructed of heavy vinyl and completely waterproof. A hunter can even wear shoes inside the boots which make waders quite warm even in the coldest of water. The problem with hip waders is they severely limit the beach hunter to very shallow water. The depth capabilities can be improved by purchasing chest waders. They are identical to hip waders in every way but instead of ending at the hip, continue up to chest level. Either style of wader can be quite warm, assuming the hunter wears well-insulated clothes underneath.

For the beginner, they are an excellent piece of gear and are reasonably inexpensive.

When hunting with waders it's necessary to use a pair of rubber gloves. The longer the better in order to allow him to dip up to the elbow. To help hold the gloves up and prevent slipping use a single suspender attached to each glove and slipped across the shoulders. It works very well.

The next step is the wet suit. Admittedly, they are a lot more expensive than waders. But many dive shops sell used suits at great savings. A used suit will do the job just as well as a new one although it may not last as long.

Try to get an outfit where the bottom section of the suit covers the entire body up to the chest and then straps over the shoulders. Once the jacket is put on, this oufit gives double insulation above the waistline where it is needed most.

Most beach hunters prefer the wet suits over waders basically because it allows them more mobility. Let's face it, water slows down the progress of a human body enough as it is without having more drag added by equipment. The streamlined wet suit allows the hunter much more freedom and speed than bulky hip waders.

Specially manufactured gloves and boots must be obtained with the wet suit. Made of the same rubber material, they work well to seal off the majority of seepage. Treasure hunters have found that mitten type gloves are vastly superior to the separated finger version when it comes to thermal quality. Keep in mind any dive shop will be more than willing to help you choose the right combination.

Perhaps the Roll's Royce of the beach hunter's gear is an outfit referred to as a uni or dry suit. This is truly the finest suit a hunter can obtain. The one piece design makes a uni completely water tight and allows the hunter to even wear street clothes underneath. When the search is over, he can simply slip out of the uni, fully dressed and completely dry.

Special gloves designed solely for the dry suit form a waterproof seal at the wristline. The hands remain quite warm even in the dead of winter.

Because the uni suit is rather expensive, it's best to have the outfit custom made to your measurements. A dive shop will order the suit for you from the factory where it will be tailored made to your liking.

METAL DETECTORS

The recent advancements in electronic technology have opened up a new world for the metal detector enthusiast. Tremendous break

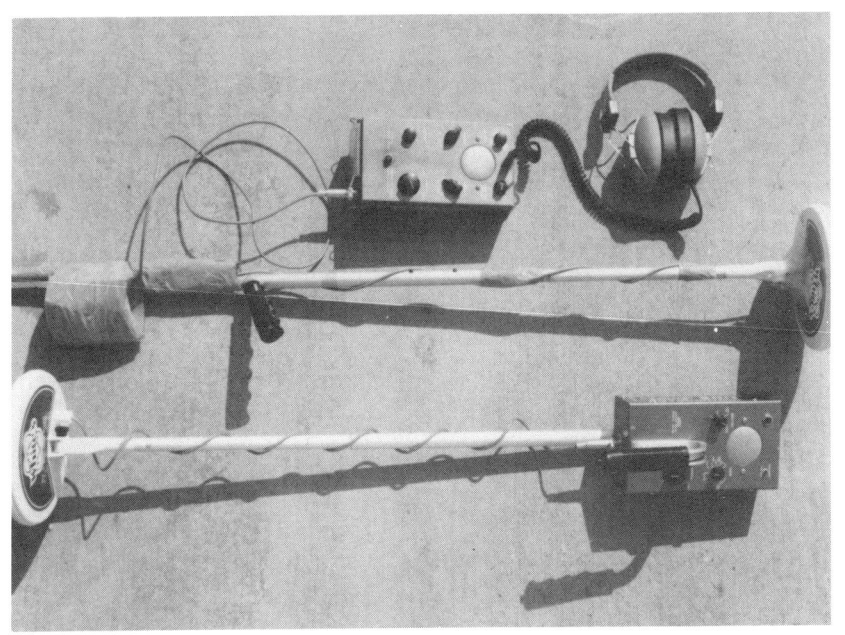

(above) The versatile hip or chest mount detector.
(below) The simple hand held version.

throughs in the discrimination modes of detection allow hunters to bypass the majority of trash. This is especially helpful to the beach hunter since retrieving a find in the water is a bit more difficult than on land. Keeping trash to a minimum saves a lot of time and energy.

Perhaps the most important factor in the ability of a detector to function properly underwater is the tuning. There are many machines that cannot be properly tuned when used at the beach. Although they work very well on dry land and are equipped with a waterproof loop they become extremely erratic when exposed to water conditions. A good water machine should be able to hold a slight tone for a reasonable amount of time before having to be retuned by the operator.

The most popular detector used at beaches today works on the Transmitter-Receiver (TR) principal. This kind of machine seems most capable of handling ground conditions below the water surface. Fortunately for the beach hunter there are a wide range of models offered by manufacturers. A basic unit can be purchased rather inexpensively and easily adapted for searching underwater.

Of course, if a hunter decides to buy a detector that is manufactured strictly for water searching he is probably buying the best machine for that purpose. Although production is now rather limited, the underwater detector is the most practical device for the serious hunter and will certainly be the machine of the future. Because the unit is completely waterproof, the maintenance required to keep it in top condition is minimal. This kind of detector is literally inpervious to the effects of water conditions and will easily outlive units that are not necessarily manufactured with beach hunting in mind.

A good second choice for the prospective beach hunter is a unit described as a hip mount or chest mount. This variation of detection design is the most versatile and requires very minimal adaptations for searching underwater. The main advantage here lies in the separation between the detector box and the shaft that holds the loop. This allows a hunter to either carry the detector strapped around his neck and lying against the chest or to mount the machine on some kind of floatation device. Remember, the detector box is not waterproof. It must be separated from the water at all times. When using the chest mount machine a hunter should always cover the unit with a plastic bag. When floating the unit or leaving it on the chest, there's a good chance water will splash against the box. The plastic bag protects the unit against possible water damage to the circuitry.

There are a few different variations for floating a detector. Most hunters use an innertube. A tube definitely has more than enough bouyancy for the job and performs much better than a styrofoam floatation device. Although some hunters use the latter, a innertube is a more practical device.

The simplest mounting technique is to rope or strap a wooden platform over the tube hole and secure the detector to the platform. Of course, any float must be tied to the hunter's waist and the optimum distance between hunter and float is about two feet.

A big advantage in using an innertube is that a hunter also has the option of converting the hole into a sifting screen. We will discuss the merits of the screen later in this chapter. However, it is basically a catch-all system that quickly separates sand or small gravel from the find. In order to construct this rig a hunter has one of two choices. He can either mount the detector to the side of the innertube or build a pyramid style platform above the tube. Both variations leave the center of the innertube free to use as a sifting screen. Simply build a frame of light wood and attach a 1/2" chicken wire screen. Then use four pieces of rope to strap the screen to the underside of the innertube at each corner.

There are no right or wrong designs for building a floating detector unit providing the system works. It's best for a prospective hunter to study the photographs provided in this chapter and choose the set up

a float combining detector and sifting screen.

most appealing to him. Since the styles of detectors differ, a hunter will have to construct the float and determine the proper dimensions based on the detector he owns. The photographs supplied here are meant to give him a good foundation to work from.

An alternative to the float is now offered by a number of manufacturers. Just as divers have cameras encased in waterproof plastic for underwater photography, the same setup can be used for a metal detector. Your local skin diving shop can have a detector waterproofed in a plastic case where the control knobs are remounted outside the plastic. This setup really performs well.

The question may cross your mind as to why a hunter would have a detector encased if he can buy a water machine already pre-manufactured in this style. What many beach hunters have discovered is that they may prefer the performance of a certain detector even though the unit is not rigged for water searching. The way that particular machine operates and appeals to him warrants having it waterproofed. It's basically a matter of preferance.

The regular hand held metal detector, where the control box is attached to the loop shaft, can be adapted for water searching. However,

In basic gear, a hunter gazes at a quarter nestled in his scoop.

there is one major drawback here. If a hunter wishes to hunt in deeper water, he has to detach the box from the shaft and mount the machine on a float or wear it as a chest mount. The problem here arises from the fact that most detectors of this design have a very short cord between the box and loop. Usually it is not long enough to allow the hunter to wear it as a chest mount or float it. There are two solutions here. He may choose to splice and add more cord to the existing line or purchase a new loop with a longer cord from the manufacturer. Most detector companies produce loops like this. It's probably best to avoid a homemade splice because waterproofing the new connection can be risky. A small trickle of water can actually ruin the loop permanently.

Although a hunter would be severely limited to shallow water, a regular hand held detector can be used as is, as long as the control box does not touch the water. Always wrap the box in a plastic bag for extra safety.

A few years ago an ingenious beach hunter devised a water detector where the electronics were mounted in the top of a hard hat. Two holes were drilled in the hat. One in the front where he mounted the tuning knob and a hole in the back where the loop cord came thru. This machine is extremely practical and hunters have incorporated this design with many different makes of detectors. Although strictly a homemade rig, this unique detector has proved very successful and surprisingly inexpensive to build.

After the decision has been made as to what kind of rig will be used there are a couple of minor changes to the detector shaft that make the hunting technique much easier. Manufacturers design the shafts for one arm operation, but this can become very tiring. To eleviate this, an extension should be added. Even a piece as simple as a broom handle or a metal pipe can be added. By simply laying the extension piece firmly beside the shaft and heavily taping or bolting the two together a hunter is then able to use the search loop in the same manner he would sweep a floor. The total length of the modified shaft should come up to slightly below the chin.

Contrary to diving, the search loop of the detector does not have to be weighted. In fact it's to the hunter's advantage to leave this loop as bouyant as possible. After a signal is pinpointed and a hunter attempts to retrieve the find he needs both hands free to use his digger. A bouyant loop will float to the surface beside the hunter, however, the shaft will remain submerged below the waterline. To correct this, a piece of styrofoam should be attached to the shaft about a foot below the top of the extension piece. A small plastic bottle with a tight sealing screw cap can also be used. If the shaft has an arm rest the styrofoam can be neatly nestled inside and taped firmly. If not, a base for the styrofoam to be attached to can be made with a small piece of wood. This adaptation will allow the loop and shaft to float peacefully beside the hunter while he digs and readily accessible for more searching once the target has been recovered.

One important point to remember is that not all search loops are waterproof. Although the vast majority of detector manufacturers have included this kind of loop as a standard feature, some do not. Make sure the machine you have or decide to purchase is equipped with a waterproof search loop before you try it out at the beach and stand the chance of ruining it for good.

When purchasing a detector always make sure a plastic search loop cover is included. If your machine does not have one get one. This useful item, easily mistaken for a frisbee, slips firmly over the bottom of the loop and protects it from excessive wear. A detector loop constantly being abraded by sand, gravel and even large objects can easily develop hairline cracks. Obviously, these cracks cause water seepage and ultimately damage the search loop beyond repair.

Keep in mind that anyone who decides to pursue beach hunting needs a little practice before he starts recovering a lot of treasure. A metal detector is only as good as the operator.

THE RETRIEVER

Recovering a find from the water is a bit more difficult than digging on land, primarily because a hunter cannot see the bottom. It takes some practice but once the technique is mastered it becomes routine. A good hunter can pinpoint and recover a target in about 15 seconds providing the find is not deeper than the retriever can penetrate in one scoop.

There are many different retrievers that have been designed over the years by beach hunters. And in different degrees, each does the job. At this point in time, beside the simple hand scoop, there are no commercial units being produced. A hunter is left on his own to construct a homemade version.

The most basic design consists of a grain scoop or shovel blade with a number of 1/4" holes drilled thru it and then attached to a wooden or metal pole. This variation seems to work fairly well at beaches where the bottom is reasonably sandy. However, where the bottom consists of solid clay, this type of retriever does not have the durability to last over the long haul. In fact it will collapse very quickly when a hunter puts a great deal of pressure on the blade while digging.

Another simple unit consists of a coffee can with the same 1/4" holes drilled in the bottom and again attached to some kind of pole. As with the grain scoop or shovel blade, it is not a very reliable retriever and will be short lived.

At first the hunter may wish to use one of the simple rigs until he gets his feet wet. But sooner or later if he wants to do some serious digging a well constructed retriever is a neccessity.

As you can see the key here is to construct the digger as heavy duty as possible. The materials used must be able to withstand quite a bit of punishment without bending or breaking. From experience, heavy gauge aluminum or steel is the answer. A unit made with either material will last indefinitely with little or no maintenance required. And although this design takes a little work to construct, it isn't too difficult and the time and effort are well worth it. The reader will find illustrations and photographs along with detailed instructions on pages A1 and A2.

There are basically two methods for carrying a retriever in the water. If a hunter uses a float with a screen sifter he can easily lay it horizontally across the innertube and pull it along. Provided the water is not too rough, this method works well.

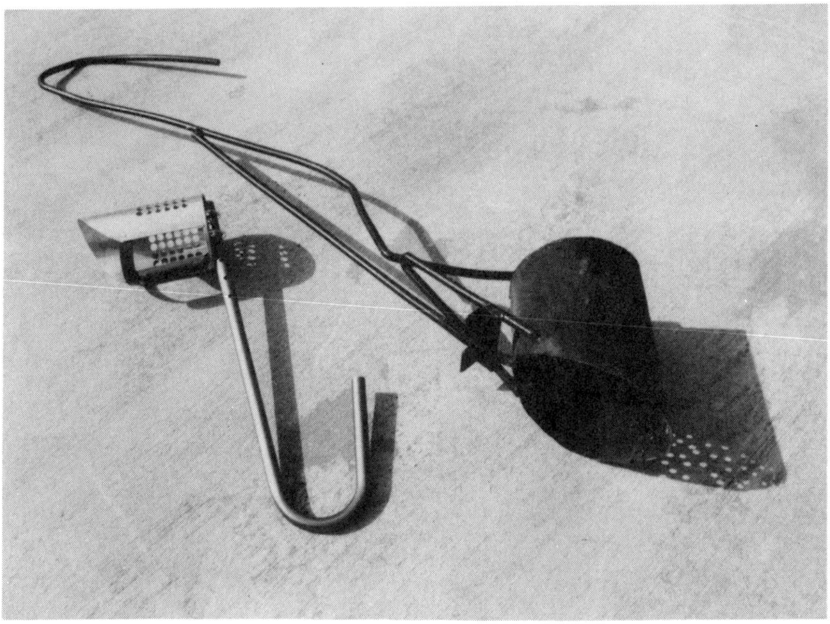

(above) A custom welded retriever.
(below) A simple hand scoop with handle attached.

Fully rigged in a dry suit and searching for treasure.

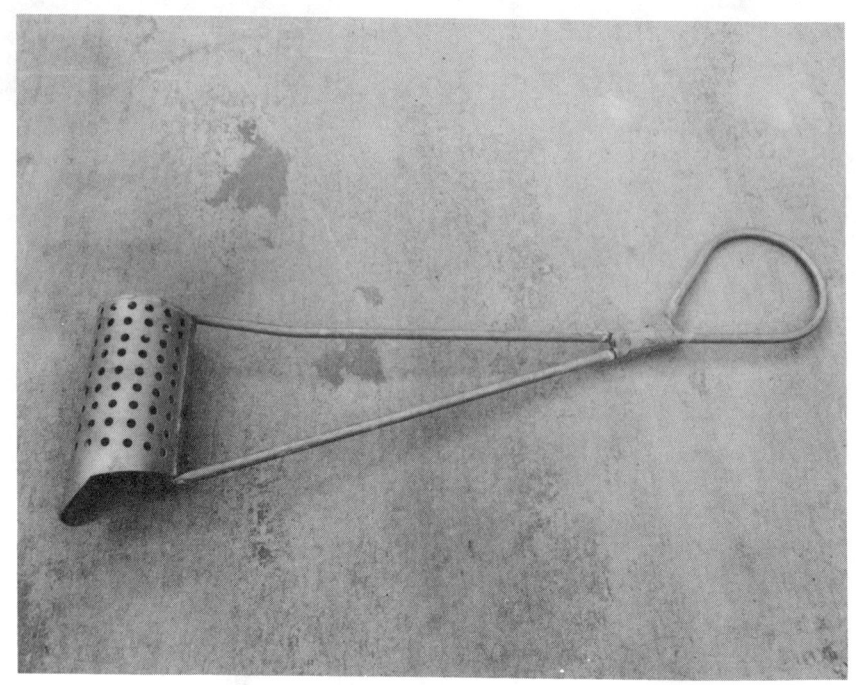

BUILDING THE RETRIEVER

STEP 1 – To construct the handle, use one 8' length of 1/2" EMT electrical tubing or reasonable substitute as in figure C. Cut tubing in two sections as in figure C. Drill three 3/8" holes in each section of tubing as shown in figures A and B.

STEP 2 – Using either steel, cast iron or aluminum, shape bucket according to dimensions in figures D and E. Drill four 3/8" holes for bolts, two on top and two on back of bucket as in diagrams D and E. Drill 1/2" sifting holes approximately 1" apart, center to center on bucket as in diagrams.

STEP 3 – Use 3/8" x 1 1/2" bolts, nuts and lock washers to assemble handle to bucket as in figure F.

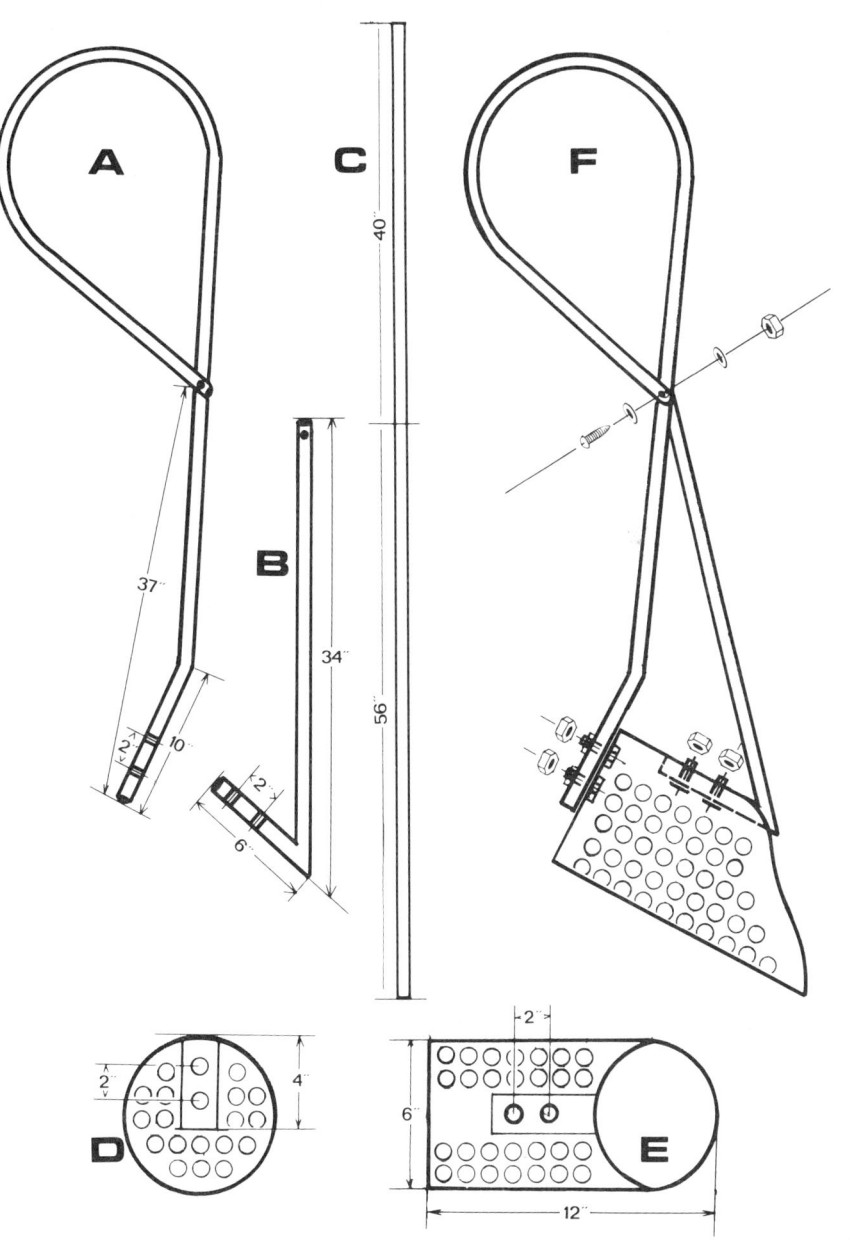

If a floatation device is not used or if the hunter prefers not to float the retriever any way, he can rig a harness out of a piece of rope. Simply slip the rope over one shoulder and then under the chest line to complete the loop. The harness can then be slipped on and off easily. Any kind of hook attached to the shaft of the retriever can be used to hang it firmly at the hunter's side.

You may even decide to carry the digger in a completely different manner. And if it works and is comfortable for you, that's all that counts.

THE SIFTING SCREEN

For many years treasure hunters have used screen sifters to separate soil, sand and gravel from valuable finds. They are extremely practical and surprisingly inexpensive. Yet at the same time, very easy to build.

These same sifters used so successfully on land have been adapted for beach searching and have cut recovery time dramatically. Although some hunters use only their retriever when separating the find from the unwanted material there seems to be no reason for it. While he must hold the digger above the water and search through it for the find a hunter who uses a sifter simply dumps the contents onto the screen. The majority of sand and gravel quickly sifts through, leaving the target easily exposed. Besides saving the beach hunter a lot of energy, it also allows him to recover treasure at a much quicker rate. He can easily out hunt the non-sifter by three to one.

Basically the water version consists of an automobile innertube with a framed piece of chicken wire strapped to the underside. This allows the wire to sit slightly below the water line which aids in the sifting action of the unit. This style sifter is so efficient that many hunters actually retrieve four or five targets before checking the screen to see what has been recovered.

Because the screen sifter is such a simple piece of gear, a hunter can put together a basic unit in about a half an hour. Simply cut a square piece of 1/2" chicken wire with a diagonal measurement to match the diameter of the innertube being used. Attach the chicken wire to a square wooden frame made simply out of four strips of wood. Finally use four pieces of rope to strap the framed wire to the underside of the tube. A hunter can then tether the floating sifter to his waistline with an additional section of rope. The distance between the hunter and the unit should be about two feet.

Although this unit works very well and has a reasonable lifespan, complete plans for a much more durable version that utilizes a motorcycle innertube can be found on pages B1 and B2. These detailed plans will allow you to build the floating sifter that the most successful beach hunters in the country are using now.

One side benefit to the screen sifter or for that matter any floatation device is that it can double as a life preserver. Even though a wader never goes in water above neck level there are still some dangers. Getting caught in a strong current caused by a ship or suddenly encountering an unexpected drop in the bottom makes the innertube a very trusty item to have beside you. Although these circumstances are rare they can happen and it's best to be prepared.

A final word of caution. Don't overinflate the innertube. Much of the gear a hunter uses has sharp edges. Inevitably the tube will come in contact with these edges and if it is overflated can easily puncture. It's much better to underinflate so that the rubber has some give.

THE FINISHING TOUCHES

As well prepared as you may be before venturing into the water, inevitably you will make some adaptations to the beach hunting gear. They will probably be minor changes to smooth out the wrinkles in your hunting operation. Basically comfort and speed are the real goals in putting together the right combination. Enjoying the hunt is an important factor in becoming successful. Being frustrated by technical failures will ultimately mean less treasure in the pocket.

Speaking of treasure, you'll need a place to keep it once you've found it. Probably the best setup is to use some kind of pouch and hang it from your neck. Make sure the one you use can easily be opened and closed, yet at the same time will not unexpectedly dump the contents back into the water. It would not be the first time a hunter has lost a handful of gold and silver under these circumstances.

Any treasure hunter who knows the first thing about metal detectors will insist on the use of headphones. This is one piece of gear that improves the depth finding capabilities of any detector. In blocking out all outside noise it greatly reduces the chances of missing a find. If you want to find more treasure get a pair of headphones.

All in all, the basic equipment from the most primitive detector in combination with a simple hand scoop can find beach treasure. It's out there for anyone with enough desire to search for it. And just as important it can be lots of fun for the beginner as well as the seasoned professional. Okay, now that we've got the equipment, let's head for the beach.

BUILDING THE SCREEN SIFTER

STEP 1 — As in diagram B, cut 4" x 3/4" soft light pine into four sections.

STEP 2 — As in diagram C, drill 1/2" holes in all four sections two inches apart as in pattern shown. Sand and reem holes for smoothness.

STEP 3— In frame style, nail four sections together with longer sections outside and shorter sections inside.

STEP 4— Cut 1/2" chicken wire to a size measuring 17" x 18 3/4" and attach to bottom of frame. To attach, either use staple type nails or secure four strips of 3/4" by 3/4" pine over wire. Screw on nail. The first choice will allow the screen to be changed in case of wear.

STEP 5— Using 50' of 3/8" rope, lace a 2.75/300-21" motorcycle innertube to the chicken wire frame as shown in figure A.

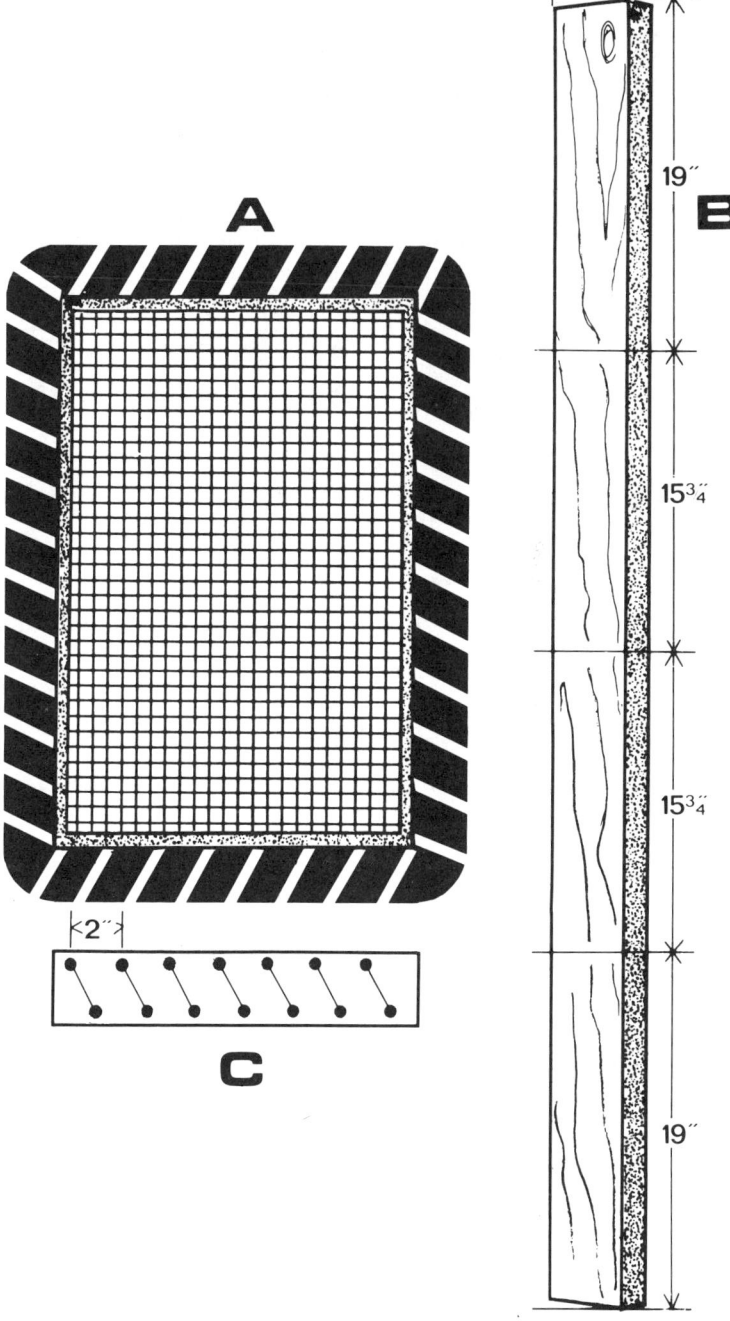

THE WHITE'S ELECTRONICS
TREASURE MASTER PI 1000

The real key to manufacturing a metal detector that performs well for the shallow water hunter is simplicity of operation. The water can be an alien environment to the beach hunter and the burden of constantly tuning and retuning the detector only adds to the difficulties of mastering underwater detection.

Fortunately, White's Electronics of Sweet Home, Oregon has gone a long way to solve this dilemma with the impressive Treasure Master PI 1000. The completely waterproof instrument with a unique mechanical vibrating sound system is literally as easy to tune as one, two, three. The simple three step tuning process can be accomplished in a matter of seconds by rotating the master control switch clockwise. Position one will check your battery. Position two will tune the PI 1000. Turn the control to position three and the instrument is ready to operate.

Because the PI 1000 utilizes a pulse induction system, the bottom stability is not affected by the majority of mineralized earth. When this detector needs to be retuned, and that's not very often, simply switch back into the tuning phase for a few seconds and then back into the operate position. Once again the PI 1000 is ready to perform, locating coins and jewelry at depths that will excite even the most demanding beach hunter.

Hats off to White's Electronics. Hunting the shallow water is as simple as one, two, three!

CHAPTER 3

TIDE AND WEATHER CONDITIONS

On a warm day in July 1715, a treasure laden fleet of ships set sail for Spain transporting a cargo of inconceivable value. Gold, silver and priceless jewelry contributed to a shipment far more valuable than had ever been loaded aboard seagoing vessels. The armada slipped peacefully from the waters of Havana Harbor under clear skys and gentle breezes. Although this fleet was the pride of Spain, one week later ten of the eleven ships would be devastated by one of the strongest forces on earth, a hurricane. With winds approaching one hundred miles an hour the vessels would be splintered beyond recognition along the Florida coast, spilling priceless treasure and artifacts along the sandy bottom.

Most any treasure hunter has heard or read the story of the fate of the 1715 Spanish fleet. And it's without a doubt one of the most amazing treasure stories ever told. But the real lesson to be learned here is the tremendous effects rendered to our planet by the constantly changing weather patterns. The effects can be devastating yet at the same time tranquil and unchanging.

For the beach hunter, weather conditions are the single most important factor effecting the chances of recovering treasure. Even the most sophisticated gear can be rendered useless when mother nature decides to act adversely. A beach may one day yield rings and coins routinely and yet the next day when weather conditions change is lucky to allow the hunter a few pennies.

The solution here lies in knowing weather patterns and their effect on swimming beaches. Lakes of course are the exception to the rule. Aside from radical weather changes such as gale force winds the bottom remains basically calm. When an article of value is lost by a swimmer it simply falls to the bottom and slowly sinks into the sand where it remains buried. Only under very high winds will the article move.

Lake beaches can contain a great deal of lost treasure and the calm waters allow the hunter easy pickings. But the problem here arises when the lake bottom consists of heavy sand. Although the lost valuables are there, they sink very quickly and within a short period of time are too deep to be located with a metal detector. Fortunately, not all lakes have loose sandy bottoms and the majority can be hunted easily without concern for weather.

The effects of mother nature really come into consideration when the beaches are located on the ocean or any tributaries. Large lakes such as Superior or Michigan also fall into this category. Although they have no access to the main water bodies of our planet, their size alone causes variation of bottom conditions in relation to weather. You might consider anyone of the great lakes as a small ocean in itself.

Beyond a doubt the tremendous amount of treasure lost in the past and being lost today at ocean resorts is beyond comprehension. At many beaches, hotels and motels stretch for miles and the swimming season attracts visitors in staggering numbers. Atlantic City, Wildwood, Coney Island and Myrtle Beach are just a few of the East coast resorts that have packed in the tourists for many decades. Even so, the Florida and California coastlines probably provide the most treasure laden beaches in the USA. Anyone with access to our ocean waters and a metal detector has access to a potential gold mine.

Even though these beaches are truly the treasure depot of all possible sites, the access is quite limited. Mother nature has a tendency to spoil the best laid plans of mice and men. So as beach hunters we must be overly patient when planning an ocean hunt. The basic reasoning is quite simple. The sheer force of the waters, even on an average day are more than a hunter or his equipment can bear. When a typical wave reaches it's breaking point even the most durable gear can be damaged beyond repair. Experience has shown that there is no match for the awesome forces of the ocean waters.

However, there are certain weather conditions that allow the beach hunter access to ocean treasure. Although he must be patient and wait for the opportune time, when it occurs, the valuables that can be recovered are mind boggling. Fifty gold rings in a single day are not out of the question.

The key here is to watch for heavy winds from a direction where they will be blowing directly off the beach. These winds should be at least 30 mph, with ocassional higher gusts. Basically, the stronger the better. What will occur is a confrontation between two forces. The heavy breakers forcing their way toward shore will be neutralized by the direct winds. At times this phenomenon can be truly amazing to witness as the ocean becomes as tranquil as a mountain lake. Granted, this is a real treat and quite a rarity, but it does occur.

The majority of the time, however, the winds are just strong enough to make the hunting tolerable. And even then the waves can be very punishing.

There is another factor that contributes a great deal to the success of ocean hunting, the tides. Our oceans, seas, and all tributaries are subject to tidal changes. Lakes are not.

The moon is the principal cause of tides. It exerts a gravitational pull on our planet. When the moon is directly over a particular area it causes a high spot in the water level. At the exact same time the spot precisely on the opposite side of earth also experiences a high water level. All scientific jargon aside, what this boils down to is that the water level will rise and fall approximately every six hours. But keep in mind that this is a rotating time schedule. For instance, the high tide one day will be about 50 minutes later the next day and will continue to rotate.

Why are tides so important when it comes to beach hunting? The answer is access. The lower the water the more area a hunter can cover without reaching neck level. Access to this extra searching territory can mean more treasure. This is especially meaningful when searching ocean territory. At high tide the water level increases so dramatically that hunting is nearly out of the question. The low water level allows the hunter more distance and also reduces the force of the breakers. From experience the best time to hit ocean beach waters is the four hour period that includes two hours before and two hours after the low tide level. Although this may seem like a short period, if the conditions are right the ocean can yield more than enough treasure in that time.

If everything falls into place properly the wind and tides will cause the bottom to form a trough a short distance from the shoreline. This trough will collect just about anything from trash to diamond rings. If you locate this bottom abnormality you are all but guaranteed a fine day's hunt.

Hunting the ocean resorts isn't really recommended for the beginner. Get some experience in less hostile waters before venturing into heavy surf. You should be able to hunt lakes and back bay beaches successfully before making the attempt.

Beaches located on bays, rivers, creeks and coves are probably the best all around swimming sites. Although these beaches are not as popular as they once were, the amount of treasure that was lost in their hey day is truly amazing. They are affected by the same weather conditions and tides that change the ocean resorts so dramatically, but on a greatly reduced scale. They rarely, if ever produce waves as large as those at the ocean.

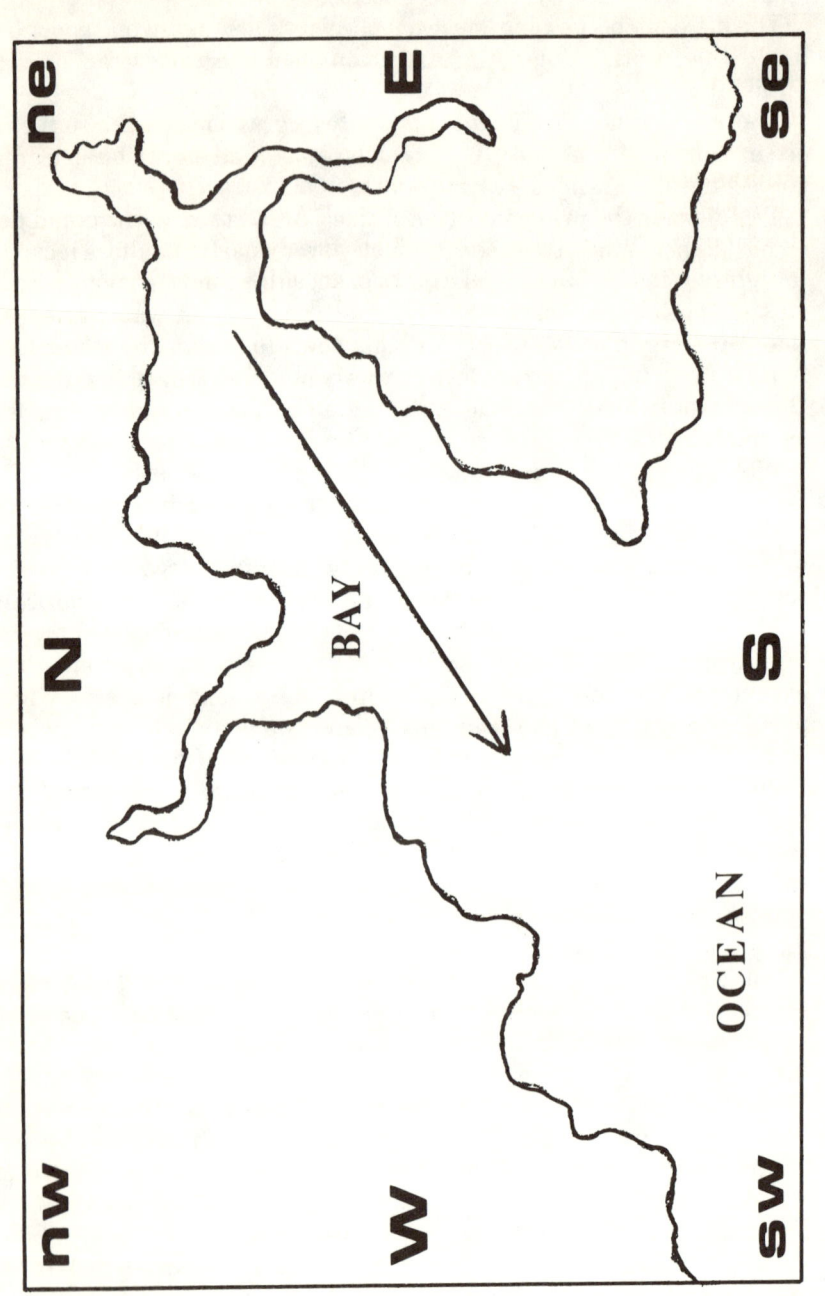

In this imaginary bay, winds from the northeast will lower the water level.

Although there are no real concrete rules concerning weather patterns and their effects on bay and back bay beaches, we can follow a number of guidelines that prove reliable most of the time. With all the sophisticated weather forecasting techniques used by meteorologists today there is still a fair margin of error. It's obvious that treasure hunters do not have access to the same equipment necessary to accurately forecast changes in the water's bottom. So as a rule, he has to go with the odds and many times rely on a bit of instinct.

First of all, let's talk about water level. As opposed to the ocean the difference in high and low tides are not nearly as great. But never the less the change is important. Most hunters will agree that the six hour span from three hours before and three hours after low tide is the best time to hunt. This isn't to say that teasure can't be found around the clock. It's always there. But the difference is a hunter will be much more comfortable searching a beach at waist level than at neck level. The hunting operation is less fatiguing when the water depth is within reason.

The tides are not the only factor that affects the level of beach waters. In fact dramatic highs and lows are primarily caused by winds. The direction of the wind and the velocity are the keys here. To determine the direction the wind must blow in order to lower the water level, one must trace the river, creek or cove to the final inland waterway before joining the ocean. Cove to creek, creek to river, river to bay, bay to ocean for example. In this example the bay is the final tributary. Therefore, simply by eyeing a map a hunter can determine the wind direction that blows from the back of the bay to the mouth. The wind's pushing effect holds back the normal tidal flow causing a temporary low water level. The more wind velocity, the lower the water level will drop. In cases where the winds reach extremely high velocities for a lengthy period of time the water can become so low that a hunter can actually walk from the original shoreline out quite a distance before reaching the new shore line. This is referred to as a "blowout".

When a blowout occurs it can be one of the biggest opportunities for the treasure hunter. Be aware that it happens only a few times a year at the most, but it allows a hunter the opportunity to reach new areas where he hasn't had access to in the past. Of course, this means more treasure for the taking, especially at beaches that have been hunted a great deal. Even though the beach may have been searched over for quite some time, it's just these deep spots than can contain a lot of the treasure previously missed.

Although low water is preferred there can be some good effects caused by high water. As you read previously hunting in high water is no real joy, in fact, it can be nearly impossible. But the benefits come after the

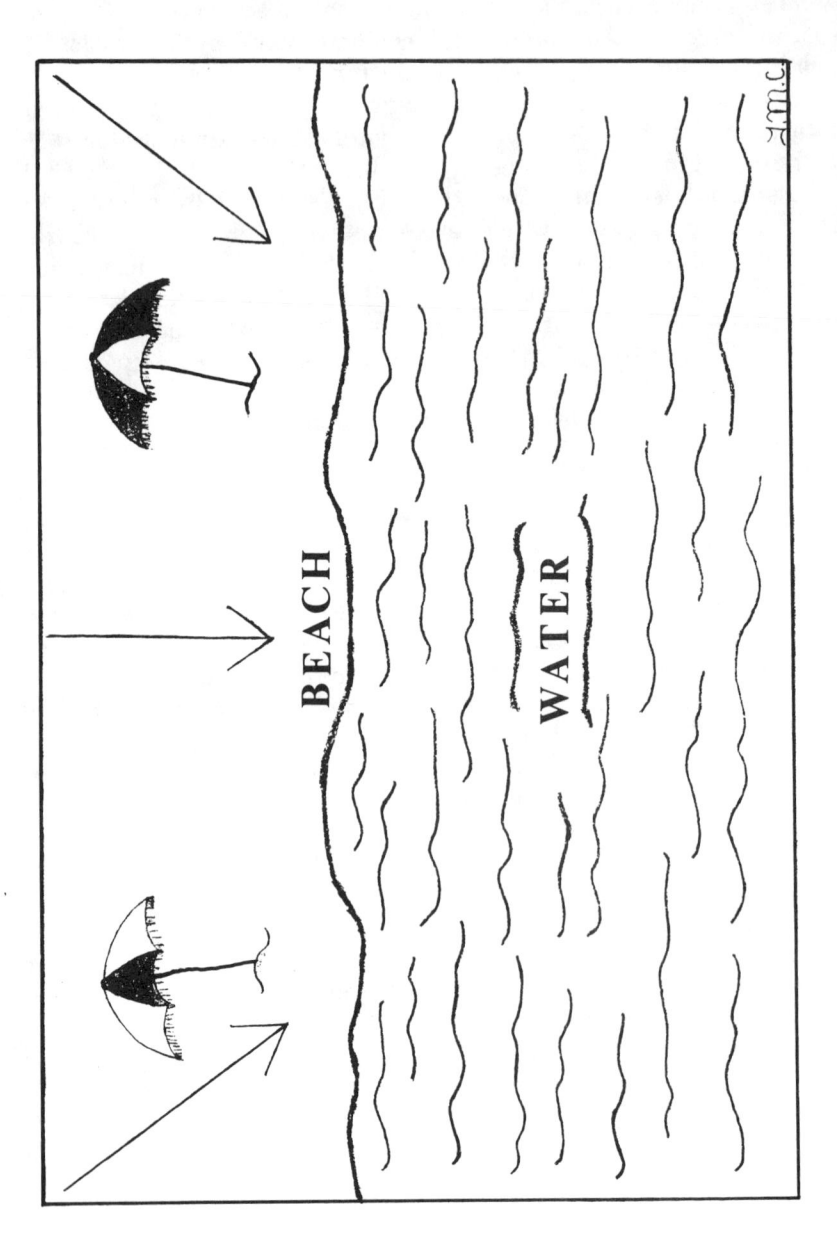

In this diagram the arrows indicate direction of moderate winds most beneficial to the beach hunter.

level subsides. What we are looking for is a higher than normal water level for a period of time and then followed by a good low. As the water level rises it is usually caused by winds blowing into shore. These winds in combination with the higher level have a tendancy to carry lost articles from quite a distance out up closer to shore. When the water level drops back down the treasure does not go back out with the tide. Reason would tell us that reversing the weather patterns would cause lost articles to return to the distance they were originally from shore. But this does not occur. As with many effects of mother nature the reasons are not fully understood at this point.

If an unusually high water level affects the shoreline in a certain manner it can also cause what is known as a "cut out". Once the water level subsides it can be recognized as a miniature cliff caused by an abrupt erosion of sand at the shoreline. The drop can be quite dramatic, at times up to three feet or more.

Imagine the amount of treasure that remains deeply buried at the sandy shoreline beyond the reach of metal detectors. The cut out effect actually erodes the treasure out and scatters it in the shallow waters of the surf where it can easily be recovered by the beach hunter. Never pass up a cut out. It's a great chance to fill your pouch with gold and silver.

Contrary to popular belief, storms are not necessarily a blessing to the beach hunter. In fact, most of the time they are a curse. To clarify this, it's important not to confuse the positive effects of a storm on the beach itself with the effects from the waterline out. Treasure hunters who specialize in land recoveries keep a watchful eye for heavy storms, basically because they push lost valuables from under water up onto the beach. This is great for the land hunter but what hurts the water hunter is that the tremendously strong undercurrents also push vast amounts of sand toward shore burying a great deal of treasure. It takes quite some time for the shoreline to return to normal after a heavy storm.

On the average, storms hurt the water hunter because they usually come from off shore in. Every once in a while one may come from the shoreline out and this can be beneficial. But they aren't that common.

Storms, cutouts, and blowouts are all occasional occurrences. They don't happen every day although they occur consistently. On the average calm day a beach can be a real joy to hunt. From experience a gentle offshore breeze can cause the bottom to yield a lot of treasure even though nothing radical is happening. Never underestimate the power of even the mildest weather conditions.

As you can see, if a hunter searches only lakes, weather and tides have no real effect. Ocean resorts, bay and back bay beaches change because weather and tides move the bottom and consequently move the treasure at the same time. That's one good reason why searching the waters of a beach will yield treasure time and time again. Even abandoned beaches where swimmers no longer provide the supply, a hunter can go in one day and feel he has covered every inch of the bottom. But the next day he may return to find an entire new load of lost articles. The wind and tide conditions simply rearrange the bottom and bring more treasure within the hunter's reach. Of course, if the beach is abandoned and no longer in use, the treasure won't last forever, but a good hunter will move onto better things long before the beach will ever be tapped out.

Keep in mind that there are many valuable sources at the beach hunter's disposal for competing with mother nature. A simple phone call to the weather bureau, the local newspapers and published tide charts are just a few of the tools a beach hunter uses to analyze weather conditions.

Above all, understand that the best way to learn about nature's effects on beach sites is to be out there hunting. Experience is the great teacher. There are just too many variables to accurately predict cause and effect one hundred percent. The section of the country a hunter does his searching can be quite different than an area a few hundred miles away. Learning the waters you are hunting takes time, but the time invested pays off in big treasure.

One final thought. If you enjoy treasure hunting on land don't ever consider giving it up. There will be days when the beach just won't cooperate and hunting is impossible. A little research and few hot spots kept in the back of your mind will make a land hunt a good alternative. Any successful treasure hunter, whether amateur or professional plays all angles. Besides, a little bit of variety makes the treasure hunting game a lot more fun.

CHAPTER 4

THE HUNT

Wouldn't it be nice if you had your own personal money tree? Or how about a pot of gold at the end of the rainbow? You'd simply go there when you needed money and pick up a basket full. Sounds great and most people dream about it all the time. Unfortunately, dreaming about it won't make it happen. Successful treasure hunters turn dreams into reality with determination and a real thrill for the game.

People basically fall into one of three categories. First of all, the scoffers who believe treasure hunting, either as a hobby or for a living is a big waste of time. They still operate under the assumption that the earth is flat. Our second type, known as the armchair treasure hunter likes the idea and gets a real kick reading romantic treasure stories and books like this one. But he'll never experience the excitement of finding treasure because he wastes too much time talking about it. And finally we come down to the devoted treasure enthusiast. He's a man like Mel Fischer or the late Kip Wagner who turned their dreams into a big treasure reality. But he is also the beach hunter who rises at the crack of dawn on a Saturday morning to scour the shoreline with metal detector in hand. More than not, his determination will make him successful. He is a doer.

There are very few sections of our country where public or private beaches are not close by. Swimming is one of our favorite pastimes and that popularity in the 20th century spurred the great beach boom. There's no lack of good beach sites for the determined hunter.

So our next step is to become familiar with the techniques of searching for and recovering water treasure. Being well equipped is important, but knowing how to use it to the best advantage separates the mediocre hunter from the real pro.

It takes a little time to become oriented to the water style. It's a lot different than land hunting, but the learning process is relatively quick and easy.

After you arrive at the beach and unpack your gear don't plunge in headfirst and start bouncing around like a grasshopper. Take time to survey the situation. Where are the winds coming from? Is the water high or low? Is the shoreline smooth or has it been "cutout"? Answering these questions will give the hunter a plan of action. For instance, if a cutout is present, hit the shoreline hard and search for the articles torn out of the sand by this effect. Then hunt the rest of the beach.

If the water level is lower than usual, head for deeper water. You can always come in closer as the water level rises. But get those targets at a distance first. Always analyze the weather and tide conditions, then make your move.

If this is a hunter's first time at a particular beach, it will be important to get a feel of the layout. Try to determine where the majority of the swimming takes place. Jetties and diving platforms are excellent clues.

If the beach has been deserted or abandoned for several years reconstructing the original layout in your mind may not be easy. A lot of times it's necessary to work from a trial and error standpoint, to discover where the main swimming took place.

Once you and your gear are in the water and comfortable, tune your metal detector to the bottom and begin searching. If the hunter uses a regular hand machine, he will be limited to the shallow water and one arm operation. Using a hip mount version or a prefab water machine will allow you to get around a bit. Grip the extended shaft firmly in front of you, keeping the detector loop flush with the bottom. As if you were sweeping the floor, slide the loop back and forth from side to side as you proceed.

Most new hunters are surprised at the number of hits they encounter so quickly. But this is par for the course. There's plenty to be found.

If the metal detector you use has a discrimination mode this adds an entirely different dimension to the search. One of the most frequent questions asked by beginners is, "How much discrimination and when should it be used?" And there are quite a few different schools of thought. Somewhere between all the varied opinions are a few reasonable rules to follow. Under normal hunting conditions it's best to use the discrimination at the level where tin foil is eliminated, but no higher. Most detectors, while having the capability to eliminate pull tabs and screw caps, will also fail to hit nickels and gold rings at that setting.

There are two exceptions to this, however. In an especially trashy area of a beach where the hunting becomes nearly impossible because of the concentration of garbage, a hunter might as well tune the discrimination to the highest level. Although he will lose the gold ring, it's better to dig coins than nothing at all. Keep in mind that detector technology is

A gold wedding band comes to the surface.

on the move and some manufacturers are claiming that new discrimination designs are in the making to solve this situation.

When searching areas that seem unusually trash free you can cut down the discrimination to the zero level. Doing this can increase the depth capabilities of your machine and help reach those heavy school rings that sink so deep. Aside from these two basic exceptions, try to keep the discrimination in the moderate range.

The most thorough search pattern used by experienced hunters is to head from the shoreline out and then back in again, in zigline fashion along the beach. This pattern will cover more territory in a minimum amount of time and speed up the locating of "hot spots". These are areas where rings, coins and other articles cluster together on the bottom. Never leave a hotspot until you are satisfied that it has been searched thoroughly. They have a tendency of moving. Once you decide to vacate the area it's quite possible you may not be able to relocate the spot that was really paying off. Get in the habit of being a patient and thorough water hunter.

Once a target has been located and pinpointed with the detector, take your left foot and place it diagonally across the loop. Don't press your weight. Simply rest your foot lightly so that the loop can be easily slipped out from underneath. Your foot will then mark the spot to dig. If a hunter is working in a loose bottom, one consisting mainly of sand, it's a good idea to dig the left heel in, leaving an impression. This makes a good starting point for the retriever blade.

Let the detector shaft and loop float on the surface at a distance where it won't interfere with your digging. Bring the retriever into position by placing the bucket or digging blade at your heel and across your instep. You are now ready to dig.

Lean the retriever handle forward which will set an angle on the position of the digging blade. Now move the left foot from in front of the blade. Place either foot that feels most comfortable on the back of the retrieving bucket. Unless absolutely necessary try not to kick at the back of the bucket or scoop. This might be needed when hunting in clay or an extremely solid bottom. But normally it's best to use firm pressure and work the blade smoothly down toward the target, in a pivoting motion. Try to fill the retriever as much as possible in order to increase the odds of recovering the object on the first attempt.

If a screen sifter is being used, and it is highly recommended, bring the full scoop to the surface and empty the contents on the screen. Most of the debris will fall thru the chicken wire and the object can be easily spotted. Depending on the composition of the beach bottom, at times a little shaking is necessary to break up the earth.

After the sifter has been thoroughly searched, if no metal object can be found use the metal detector to recheck the hole that was dug. Many times the hunter will have to go down more than one scoop on a deep target. It's also very easy to miss the object on the initial attempt and the detector will indicate the correct spot for a second try.

Occasionally the target cannot be found in the sifter and the detector indicates that the hole is empty. There are basically two explanations and both happen frequently. The object may be smaller than the 1/2" chicken wire and consequently falls thru and back to the bottom. Almost always the target of this size is trash. It's very unusual for a coin or piece of jewelry to measure less than 1/2". Some hunters prefer to use 1/4" chicken wire just in case, but will admit that the sifting capabilities are greatly reduced, therefore making the target much more difficult to spot once it has been recovered.

The second cause for losing a prelocated signal deals with the retriever itself. By chance the tip of the bucket blade will come in contact directly over the target and instead of digging the object, will actually

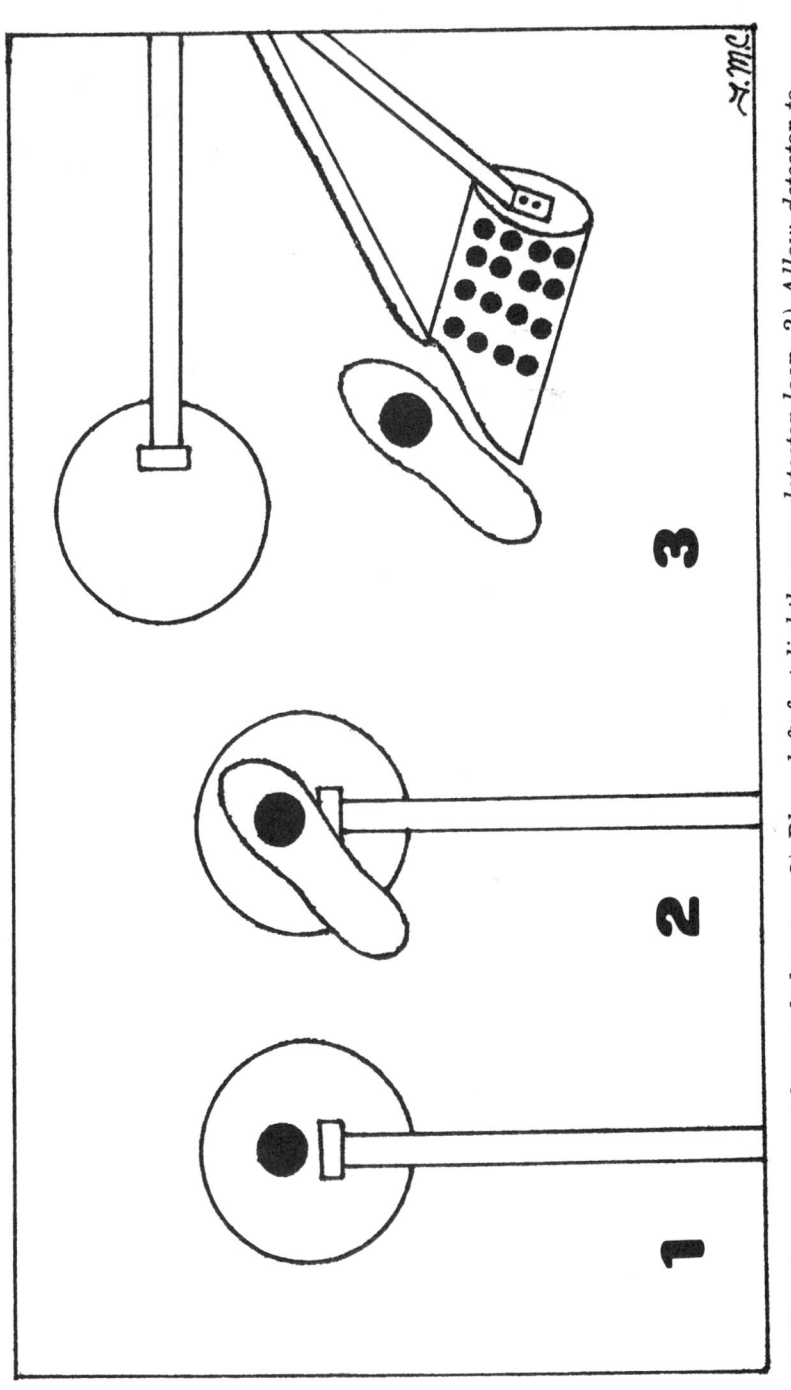

1) Pinpoint target with metal detector. 2) Place left foot lightly over detector loop. 3) Allow detector to float on surface and bring retriever bucket into digging position. Move left foot and dig.

push it much deeper into the earth. Although the metal detector does not register a signal, the target is there never-the-less, but beyond the depth penetrating power of the machine. To make sure that this is not the case take an extra dig from the hole and then recheck it with the detector. You might be surprised at finding an unexpected diamond ring in your sifter.

An interesting story related by a beach hunter recently tells the whole story. He had been recovering quite a few rings that day and was sure his signal was a ring even before he dug it. From experience he had learned to distinguish many targets strictly by ear. After his first attempt to retrieve it, the signal was lost. He tried in vain to relocate the target and after a few minutes gave up and moved on to another signal. Reaching for his retriever he was shocked to find a large gold school ring perched majestically on the bucket blade. Apparently the back of the ring had snapped leaving a gap where the retriever blade slipped in snuggly. The ring gripped the blade like a vice. What a pleasant surprise.

Always rechecking a hole for a second signal is a good habit to get in to. As was mentioned previously, coins and jewelry have a habit of clustering together on the bottom. This means that more than one article in a single hole is not unusual. In fact, many hunters have recovered three or four rings in a single scoop. The lesson to be learned here is that abandoning a hole after retrieving a single article and not double checking with the detector can be a big mistake. It really hurts when your beach hunting partner holds up a pretty gold ring and informs you that he plucked it from the hole you just left after digging a nickel.

From experience it seems that the majority of lost articles tend to collect in areas where a loose sand and gravel mixture about five inches deep rests on a clay bottom. Rings and coins are nestled in the clay and held securely by the layer on top. If the sand and gravel moves off the clay leaving it bare, the treasure doesn't stay very long. The water movement along the bottom quickly sweeps the objects like a broom until they rejoin the loose mixture.

Some heavy rings have a tendency to sink firmly in the clay bottom. They will remain in the clay for quite some time before bottom currents have enough force to erode them out. Retrieving an object stuck in the clay is a bit harder than simply digging a hole in loose bottom. It's very important to pinpoint the exact spot of the target before digging, basically because you will find that only a small hunk of clay can be dug at one time. An accurate job of pinpointing can save a lot of time and energy.

The proper digging stance.

A simple little gadget used over the years by beach hunters can be very useful for keeping track of the beach situation during a particular hunt. During the search if a certain spot begins to yield a few good items a hunter will drop a floating marker. By simply attaching a six foot piece of cord to a small square of styrofoam and securing the other end to a heavy fishing sinker, the hunter has made a transfixed buoy that he can easily spot. If by chance he wonders from the area he can routinely return to where the hits were paying off. After a hunter is satisfied that he has worked the spot thoroughly he can pack up the marker and use it later at another hot spot. Although the float is not a critical piece of gear, it can sure come in handy.

When handling treasure in the water always keep the object over the sifting screen. It can be difficult to handle small articles in the water, especially when wearing rubber gloves. If a hunter drops a piece of treasure without holding it over the screen there's a good chance he will not be able to recover it. The bottom currents can quickly sweep it off to another area. Losing a pretty piece of jewelry or fine coin can really be frustrating. Play it safe.

If you're a really smart hunter, get in the habit of taking the better finds back to your car or up on the shore line. Diamond rings are a good example. There are any number of mishaps that can occur while searching in the water. Even though the diamond is held securely in a pouch, the safest place for it is on shore.

As you can see good hunting techniques are the real key to successful beach hunting. Finding treasure is the ultimate goal, but it's also important to consider safety. Granted there is nothing exciting about safety precautions but never the less a little respect for the water can go a long way in preventing tragedy.

When weather conditions cause exceptionally rough waters a hunter has no business being there. Our oceans have an undertow forceful enough to drag a man into deep waters with no trouble, when the seas become violent. Avoid these rough weather conditions. There will be plenty of nice days to hunt along the way.

Never remain in the water when a storm is brewing. Thickening black clouds moving overhead are nothing to ignore. It goes without saying that electrical storms and water do not mix and the results could be fatal for the beach hunter who hangs around too long.

Beware of large ships running close to the coastline. The waves caused by these floating giants can feel like a tidal wave to the unsuspecting hunter. Always keep a close eye on the horizon when hunting a beach near a shipping lane. If a wave is spotted heading your way, move into water below waistline level for safety.

If you feel that these safety tips tend to paint beach hunting as a dangerous hobby, don't. With a little bit of caution any dangers can be reduced to nearly nonexistent. The basic point here is to realize the possibilities, no matter how remote they may be, and hunt in a prudent fashion. The best tragedy is one that never occurs.

When you enter the water for the first time don't be surprised if you feel a bit lost and come home empty handed. The learning process takes a little time. But don't be surprised if you come home the first day with a diamond ring either. It happens a lot.

Be persistent and have patience. If you stick with it, treasure will come your way. Although it may seem tough at first, after a few hunts are under your belt, recovering beach treasure can become quite routine.

Don't hesitate. Get your gear together and head for the beach.

CHAPTER 5

RESEARCHING SWIMMING BEACHES

A sunken wreck has been located off the coast of Florida and the search crew prepares to dive in hopes of recovering the precious cargo. Gold, silver and even jewels are all possibilities. The excitement swells in anticipation of the first days search. This is the moment everyone has waited for.

The thrill of the big treasure hunt, and the anticipation of recovery are hard to describe in terms that do them justice. But the actual hunt is only a part of the entire operation. Years of detailed research are necessary before a professional makes the decision to go after his target. Be it the land hunter in search of a buried cache or divers in search of lost wrecks, recovery is nearly impossible without thorough research.

For the big treasures it takes a lot of time to compile enough information to make a hunt feasible. Comparitively, beach hunting does not require this type of exhausting research. In fact, it's very easy. There are so many sources available to the hunter for locating swimming beaches that he might even learn to enjoy researching.

Before pursuing our possible sources, it's important to point out that not everyone has to use the research angle. For that person who is strictly out for enjoyment and pleasure while hunting, research may not be his cup of tea. Don't feel bad if that's your attitude. There's nothing wrong with pursuing treasure strictly for enjoyment. If you don't want to research, don't do it. There's still plenty of treasure to be found by simply remembering a few beaches and planning weekend hunts. Beach hunting doesn't fall in the same category as pursuing big time treasure professionally. But then again it takes a lot less time and money. Research can take time, but it isn't a prerequisite for enjoying beach hunting.

There are however, times when digging for information can really pay off. The hunter who invests a great deal of time in research, is the kind of

Ticket booth and concession stand at the gate to an old swimming beach.

person who does everything all the way. His goal is to dig lots of beach treasure and he is willing to do anything that helps, regardless of whether he enjoys it or not. He usually has quite an impressive collection to show for his efforts.

The sources at the beach hunter's finger tips are numerous. Swimming beaches are as much a part of history as a civil war battle site. Any hunter who wishes to, can easily compile an impressive array of information to help in locating swimming sites, either new or old.

Any beach can be put in one of three categories. The new beach, one that has operated since about 1965, has the least to offer. Although jewelry can be found in limited quantities, silver coins are very scarce. This is easily understood since clad coins replaced silver versions in 1965.

Beaches dating back before 1965 on the average contain much more treasure. Silver coins are plentiful since that was the medium of exchange at the time. School rings, precious gemstones and antique jewelry are abundant. Not only has the older beach had more exposure in years, but also in volume. Since the late 60's when environmental conditions became such a hot issue, the popularity of our beaches has declined. People are leery of the quality of the water. Beaches that at one time packed in visitors by droves have dwindled down to average size crowds. Hopefully this trend will change as our environment improves.

This second category of pre 1965 swimming beaches that are still in operation are also being replenished to a certain extent. Although the crowds are not what they used to be, people are still losing valuables in the same old way.

The third swimming site is one that has been abandoned. This is where good research pays off. It's surprising the number of beaches that were completely closed down in the 60's and left to ruin. It takes a little digging to find those old obscure sites, now overgrown and all but forgotten. But when you find one, the payoff can be fantastic. The abandoned beach, although no longer being replenished by swimmers has two important advantages. First and foremost, the competition among hunters is not as great as at swimming sites in current use. The average treasure hunters always flock to the obvious sites first. The good researcher who locates the forgotten spots will have a field day recovering treasure with little or no competition. The other advantage here lies in the fact that year round hunting is possible without the beach crowds. Most hunters realize that searching during the swimming season must be done early in the morning before the swimmers appear. It's not very comfortable when people are hovering close by.

By now you must be thinking of a number of swimming sites currently at your disposal. Maybe a lake or a little cove where you swam as a teenager. They can all pay off.

Let's examine a number of good sources that beach hunters have relied on over the years to supply information while researching.

The Library

Even though this source may seem a bit obvious, it can provide leads to quite a few local beaches. All libraries have a section that deals with state and local history. These books are invaluable. Some contain lengthy and detailed information about resorts, lakes, public and private beaches. Local historians pride themselves on giving details about old and abandoned swimming sites. When you find the right books the writers have basically done the research for you.

Newspapers

There's a lot more to be said for old newspapers than lining the bottom of bird cages. In fact this may be one source that supplies more leads to the hunter than any other. If for no other reason, the sheer volume of *(above and below) Both these beaches, now abandoned, are hard to recognize as swimming sites.*

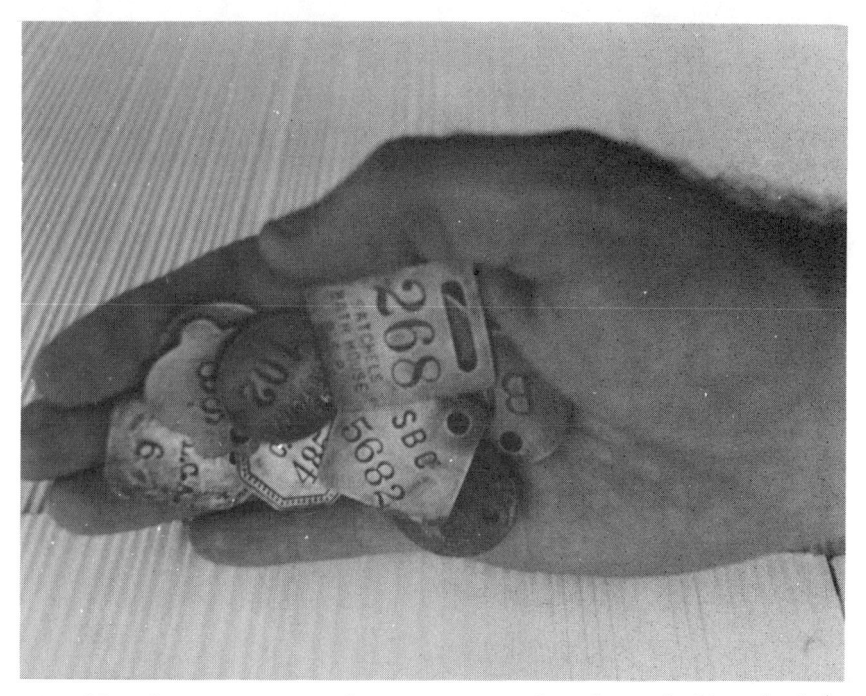

Metal beach tags were worn by swimmers and used as a clothing check for the bath house.

newspapers published over the years provides a tremendous amount of material in itself.

Most libraries carry the local newspaper on a micro-card where it can be viewed thru a special machine made for this purpose. Newspapers also have a department called the morgue where all previously published papers are either available in their original form or on micro-cards.

There are a few guidelines to follow when researching old papers. First of all go back at least to the 50's. You're looking for the older beaches. New ones are common knowledge. If you have lived in the area for any reasonable time, you know where they are. It's the older beaches, some now closed down, that you should be looking for.

Pick a particular year and only look thru the spring and summer publications. Of course, this is the time of the year when beach action begins. Look closely for advertisements hyping particular swimming sites. These ads were very common basically because there was a lot of competition for business among pay beach owners.

Wooden diving platform.

Some papers had recreational sections where you can find old articles on the beach scene, written at the time as a community service.

One last hint that may provide more info than you can imagine, the lost and found section. A typical ad might read: DIAMOND RING LOST AT BROWN'S BEACH $50 REWARD 555-1209. From this ad you know that a Brown's beach existed, people swam there and jewelry was lost. Find Brown's beach and you've found treasure. And there are many other sources at your disposal for locating that beach, if the newspaper isn't helpful.

The Department of Parks & Recreation

Every state or local government has a department that promotes and regulates recreational facilities. This includes swimming beaches. Depending on the size of the budget allotted to these departments, some are quite large and can provide quite a bit of information to the beach hunter. The best way to request materials is by writing a letter. Ask the department to send you a list of all recreational facilities that include swimming beaches on the premises. At times their lists can be quite lengthy and the department will be more than glad to mail it to you.

An old beach pavillion used to shade the picnickers.

Department of Permits

Many states and counties require that owners of swimming beaches obtain a permit before allowing anyone into the water. These permits are a matter of public record and can be seen upon request. You might want to visit this department and spend an afternoon filing thru their records. Finding old expired permits can lead to locating a forgotten beach and you might just be the first hunter in the water.

Maps

Times change, people change and the land we live on changes. Some changes are man made. Others are caused by mother nature. Either way our surroundings are not consistent, but rather in a state of constant metamorphosis.

Studying an old map is like turning back the hands of time. It's a still life picture of cities and towns, highways and roads as they were at that time. They can be the beach hunters best friend.

Very few serious hunters do not have an impressive collection of maps that span decades. They are an invaluable source for locating old swimming sites. Knowing a beach once existed is only half the way there. Finding it isn't always that easy. Maps are the solution.

College Campuses

If you are lucky enough to live close to a college or university you are probably very close to a treasure laden swimming site. Nearly every college has its "Swimmin Hole". A lake, river or cove nearby where the students hang out in the swimming season. College students wear college rings and just like anyone else they lose them quite frequently while swimming. A good place to start looking is in an old school yearbook.

Steamer Routes

During the big years of the steamboats, passengers would line up at designated points along the shoreline waiting to be picked up for afternoon excursions. During the swimming season they had their hands full transporting anxious picnickers to water playgrounds along the coast. Steamer routes can be found in many local history books and also in publications that take a nostalgic look at the steamboat as a whole. Maps that chart the steamboat routes can also be found in maritime museums.

Watermen

Imagine if you made a living as a fisherman, oysterman or crabber. The waterways would be a second home and you'd know the territory like the back of your hand. How many beaches would you spot in your travels? Dozens. Your knowledge of the coastline could provide any beach hunter with the locations of rich treasure sites.

Watermen are an excellent source of beach information for the treasure hunter. Never pass up an opportunity to talk to a man who has been active in the harvesting of seafood. The coastline is etched in his memory and he knows the locations of beaches you may have never even heard of.

Senior Citizens

Some of the best information possible can come from our senior citizens. Their experiences offer a never ending source of treasure leads.

Ask any senior citizen, "Where did you swim when you were a teenager?" and in no time you'll have more beach locations than you can handle.

For one thing our older citizens go out of their way to be helpful and really enjoy conversation. They'll be more than glad to supply you with the history of the beach scene in your area. Don't be surprised if they even mention a few rings they lost over the years. Their help can be priceless.

As you can see research is an important tool for the serious hunter and the sources available to him are numerous. Besides the sources mentioned, you can probably come up with quite a few on your own.

If you are a beginner, you are about to enter a world of adventure that few experiences can rival. From the possibility of diamond rings and gold coins to a few old pennies, the excitement in searching and finding is hard to match. What's more the beach hunter who pursues this hobby seriously has a good chance of producing a steady income. Many hunters do it for that purpose.

Be persistent and patient, but at the same time enjoy yourself. Good things usually take time and effort, but time and effort well spent. The best of luck in all your treasure hunting endeavors.

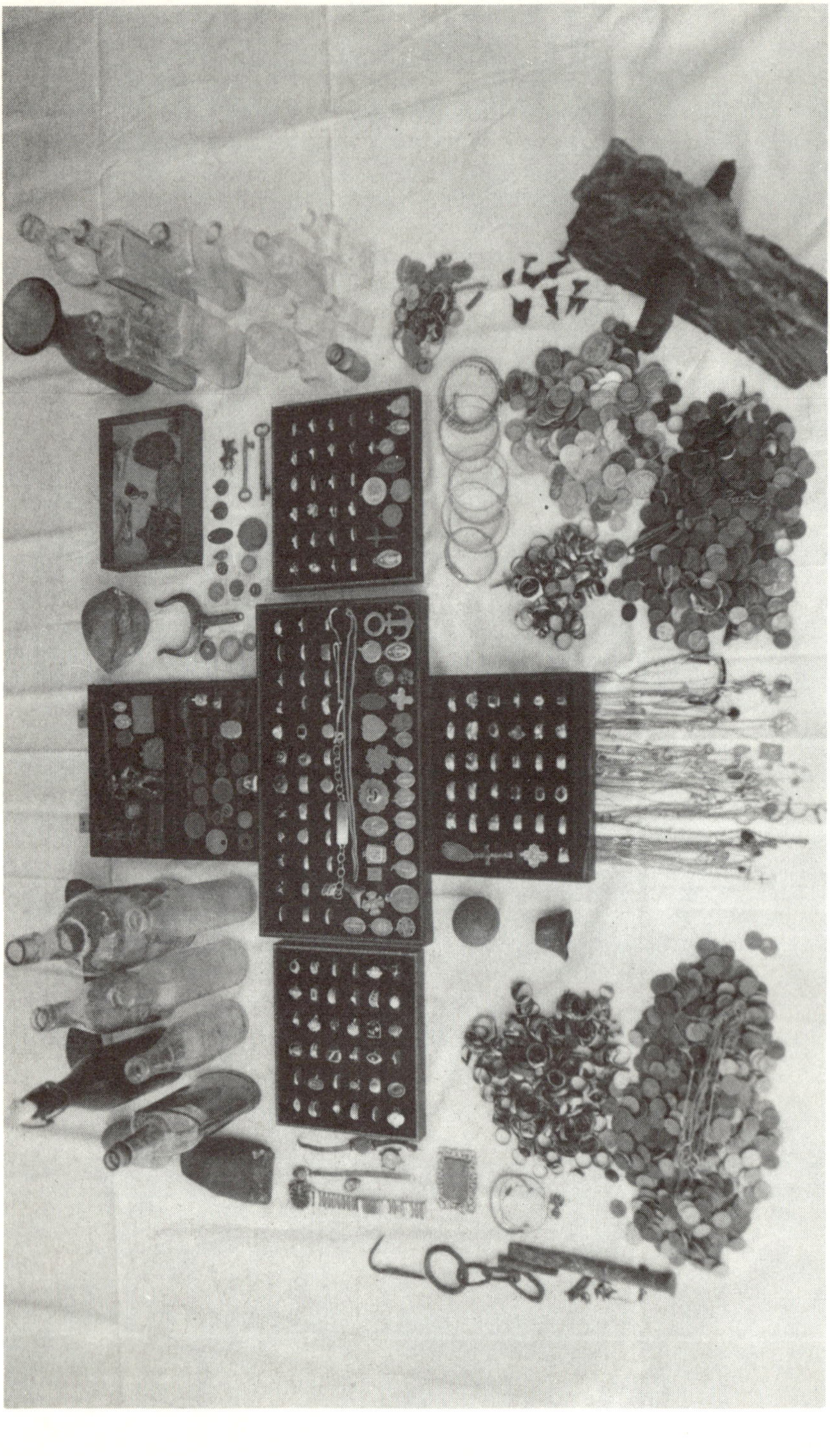

*A special thanks to S. Sanders of
Sanders Keepsake Jewelers, Glen Burnie, Maryland
for teaching a couple of amateurs a thing
or two about the world of gemology.*